DAM VIEWS

Carlos Hustle's

DAM VIEWS

A Poetry & Art Collection

by

Charles Hubbard

Mattawa, Washington

Cover photo: Charles Hubbard
Illustrations: Charles Hubbard
Interior and cover design: Gray Dog Press, Spokane, Washington

ISBN: 978-1-7324349-0-5

Twitter   @CarlosHustle509
For inquiries: motherhubbardcreative@gmail.com or
                 nonchalantcharlie@gmail.com

Printed in the United States of America

This book is dedicated to:

My wife, my daughter, my parents, and my homies,
thank you for putting up with me.

And to Hip Hop, thank you for teaching me so much.

Contents

* Includes illustration

DAM VIEWS

Intro

Art Inspires Action.
Action Inspires Art.
Take Action, Make Art.
—Charles Hubbard

Ode to Mr. Shiveley from Kamiakin Junior High

Remember when I was in your 8th Grade English Class
And you told me I couldn't write my poetry paper
About A Tribe Called Quest's
I Left My Wallet in El Segundo
Because rap music wasn't poetry?
What a dick.

CAUTION
EXPLICIT
THINKING

Parental Advisory

You can't break my will
Because it's ironclad.
That right there's something
I learned from my Dad.
You can't break my spirit
Because it's just too strong.
That right there's something
I learned from my Mom.

Start Your Engines

Fools out searching, searching,
Searching all the time.
When that which
They are searching for
Is right inside their mind.

Career Goals

Kids, I hope you get to grow up to be cowboys
And ride out on the open range
Because to live and die in a cubicle
No better than in a cage.
So learn all of you letters
And practice all your math
So that when you grow up
You can choose your own path.

#Mood RN

Don't talk to me
Don't talk to me
Hey motherfuckers
Don't talk to me.
Don't text at me
Don't message me
Don't tweet at me
Don't talk to me.
Don't voicemail me
Don't email me
Don't DM me
Don't talk to me.
Don't phone call me
Don't snap to me
Don't friend request me
Don't talk to me.
Don't facetime me
Don't IG me
Don't snail mail me
Don't talk to me.

Fuck you that's why,
I just want to think.

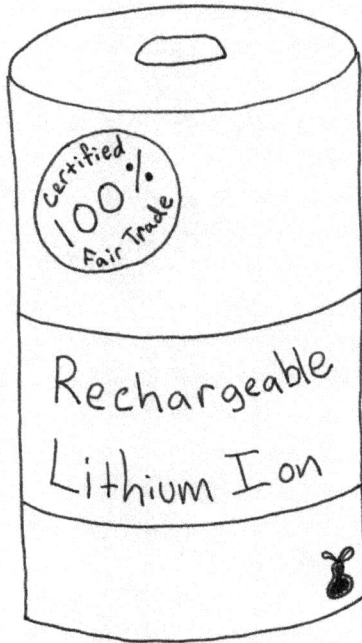

Certified 100% Fair Trade

Rechargeable Lithium Ion

Add to Cart

Status: Temporarily Unavailable

CH '18

Fair Trade Phone

A fair trade phone,
Do such things exist?
OF COURSE NOT, cause the only thing
People give two shits
About (leave politics & corporate profits out)
If you had any doubt
Was the bottom line
The dollar amount
That they have to pay to keep up with
Housewives and Kardasians
While children in the Congo stay steady smashing them
Rocks
For cobalt mineral recovery (makes battery)
Small hands pick up lots
In 12 hour days for pennies in pay
But man, don't say nothin
Cause hey,
That kills a bitches vibe
And they ain't got time for that anyway
Too many pals to pay
And dragons to slay
Ya 'ne?

12 Year Old Day Here & There

Here (USA)   There (DRC)
   \   /
    \   /

Sleeping until woken
  /   \
 /   \

By phone   By guardian
Check messages   Escorted to work
Cartoons & breakfast   Maybe eat
Check messages   Dig a tunnel
Shower dress bus   Use a shovel
Check messages   Use your hands
Boring school   Pick the cobalt
Check messages   Pile the cobalt
Lunch   Maybe eat
Check messages   Maybe not
More boring school   Maybe get beat
Check messages   Dig another tunnel
Cartoons & snacks   Use another shovel
Check messages   Use your hands again
Practice & video games   Pick the cobalt
Check messages   Pile the cobalt
Wish for a better battery   Wish for a better life
    \   /
     \   /

Stupid Phones
  /   \
 /   \

```
Check messages                    Bag the cobalt
 Charge battery                  Carry the cobalt
Check messages                   Carry the cobalt
TV boring homework               Carry the cobalt
 Check messages                    Escorted home
Dinner                               Maybe eat
 Check messages                      Maybe not
TV brush teeth                   Maybe get beat
 Check messages                  Maybe get sick
Pray for better phone          Pray for better life
                \                /
                 \              /
                      Sleep.

                     Repeat.
```

Draft 2K

What if the all first born sons and daughters
Of all the families that made over two hundred thousand dollars
Were the first to be sent to war
Instead of those born to the poor?

I wonder,
Would the politicians and industrialists be as eager
To go to war then
And put those cold bags of money
Where their children had been?

These are the things they ask us to do
Sacrifice many to benefit few.
Go die or kill for a land
Where you're not treated equal
I guess the rich just get richer
So fuck common people.

Goochi

Bigger, Better, Faster, Cheaper

More Prophets
More Profits
More Celebrations
More Corporations
More Enchantments
More Entrapments
More Consumption
More Destruction
More Buying
More Dying

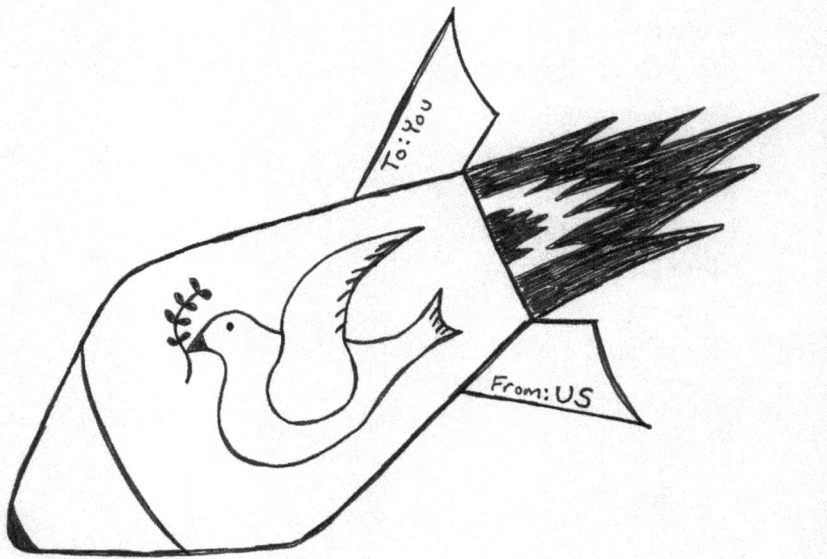

God Bless US

Take a good look and see
United States of Hypocrisy.
Do as we say
Not as we do
Bow down and hail
Red, White and Blue.
Preach world peace
But practice war,
Will doves ever fly
Where eagles soar?

Autoreplacements

I love my Computer/Smartphone/Tablet.

My Computer/Smartphone/Tablet is the most important thing I own.

My Computer/Smartphone/Tablet is my true best friend.

My Computer/Smartphone/Tablet is always there for me.

My Computer/Smartphone/Tablet helps me learn new things.

My Computer/Smartphone/Tablet helps me gain deeper understandings.

My Computer/Smartphone/Tablet entertains me when I'm bored.

My Computer/Smartphone/Tablet keeps me company when I'm lonely.

My Computer/Smartphone/Tablet helps me invent new things when I need them.

My Computer/Smartphone/ Tablet helps me be creative when I'm in the mood.

My Computer/Smartphone/Tablet is my gateway to freedom.

My Computer/Smartphone/Tablet lets me know what's going on.

My Computer/Smartphone/Tablet is something I couldn't live without.

My Computer/Smartphone/Tablet is something I depend on all day, every day.

My Computer/Smartphone/Tablet helps me find where I'm going, without it I'd be lost.

My Computer/Smartphone/Tablet is the most powerful device on the market.

My Computer/Smartphone/Tablet helps me stay organized.

My Computer/Smartphone/Tablet is my favorite thing to play with.

My Computer/Smartphone/Tablet is a valuable tool that helps me with life.

My Computer/Smartphone/Tablet is what makes me happy.

---------------->Edit:

--------------------->Autoreplace: Computer/Smartphone/Tablet with Brain

---------------------------->END.

I.G.A.F.

Everyone talking
But nobody listening.
People all start shit
Without ever finishing.
Wanna go to the party
But not help clean it up,
Things Fall Apart
When everyone DGA Fuck.

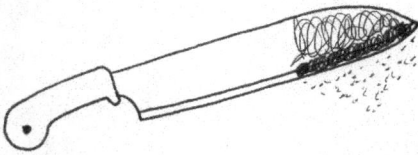

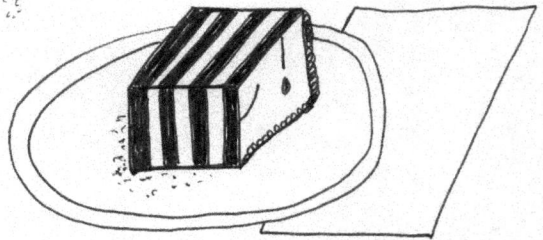

Seven Layer Life

Do it now don't wait for later
Play it loud say fuck the neighbors
Be yourself say fuck the haters
Only cook with major flavors
Only ball with major players
Flex on doubters and naysayers
Life like cake kid seven layers.

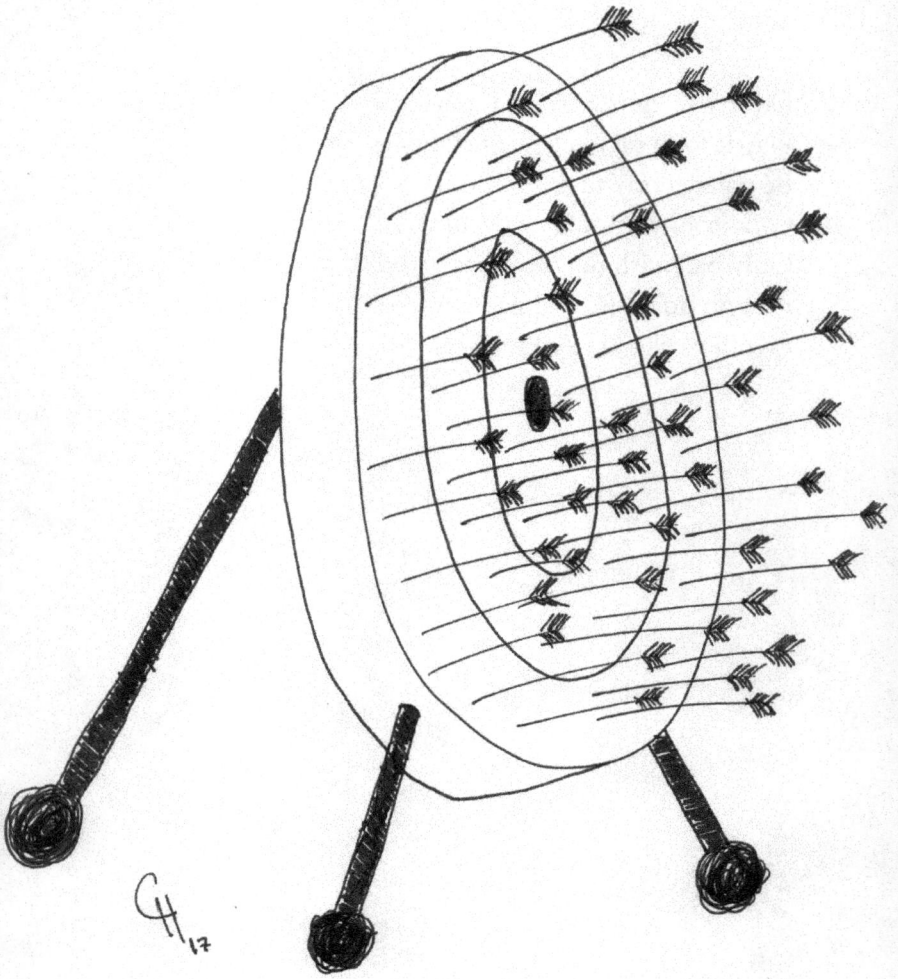

Mental Archery

The mind is the bow
The body is the arrow
Freedom is the target
Margin of error is narrow.
Aim the bow with focus
       Release,
Let the arrow leave view.
Bullseyes will be struck
When to yourself you stay true.

BIG BROS. CIRCUS

Now Showing
THE
Frightening
Free Mind

Thinkers

You think too much.
You question too much.
Thinkers & Questioners change the world.
We don't need any of those,
The world is perfect the way it is.
You think too much.

Lama Drama

Big red wall won't let me go
Big red wall won't let me home.
High in the mountains
People all alone
Continue to meditate
Continue to roam.

Next-Ex

My girlfriend thinks I'm great
But I'll be better when I change
Quit all my bad habits
And ditch my friends cause they're all lame.

Muscle Memory

When life knocks you down
Get up and hit back
That's the best thing
You can do.
No time to mope
No time to cry
No time for feeling blue.
We must realize that life is suffering
It's the same the whole world over.
Just have faith
That things will work out
Whether you worship Jesus
Allah, Buddha, or Jehova.
Things happen for reasons
We may not yet understand
But you've got to see
That these struggles
Will make you
A better woman or man.

Follower

Across the ocean
Over the sea
There is a girl
Who's waiting for me.
If I never make it
Please let her know
I follow the wind
Wherever it blows.
Over the mountains
Across this land
There is a girl
Who waits for my hand.
If I never make it
Please let her know
I follow my spirit
Wherever it goes.

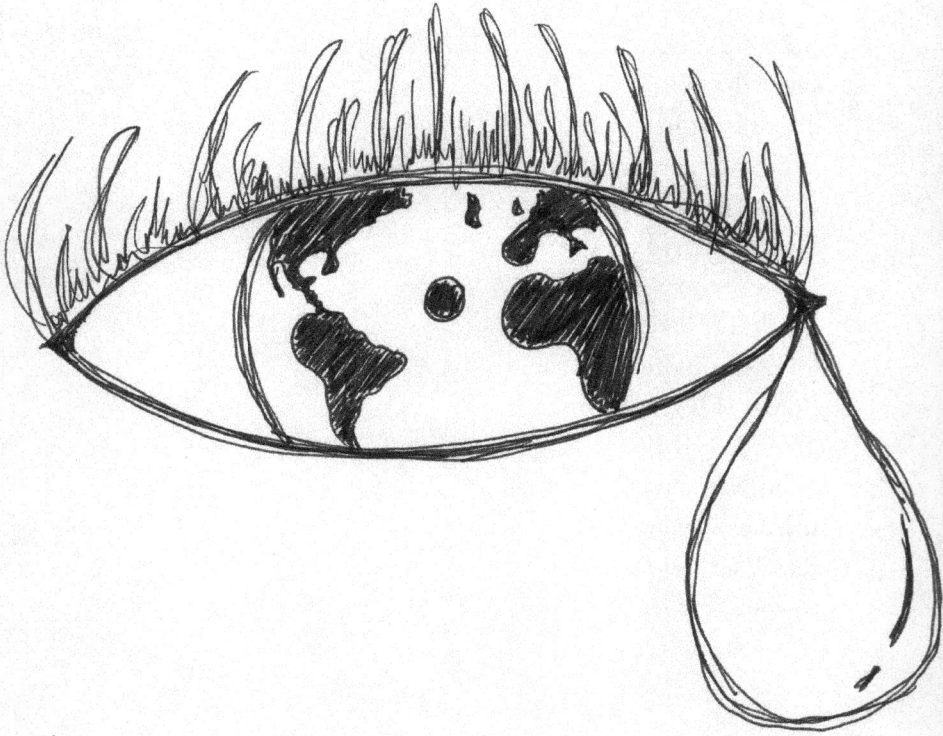

Suffering Mother

Brothers and sisters.
Sons and daughters of Earth.
Do you not hear our mother crying?
Do you not see the scars we inflict upon her face?
Do you not smell the sores festering upon her body?
Do you not feel her pain?
I feel her pain.
When I walk in the woods
Or in the mountains.
When I sit by the river
And watch the birds and fish.
She speaks to me.
Through the trees and the rocks
Through the water and the clouds.
She speaks to me
And I feel her pain.

Earth Day Limerick

Mother Earth has a cancer called humans
Her whole body they've set to consuming.
They'll use her all up
Then wonder "what the fuck",
And point fingers about whose fault it is
   that their planet was ruined.

The Human Animal

Every animal on Earth
Will have to change tactics
All because of the human animal's
Love of plastics.
And their passion for other uses
Of coal, oil, and gas.
Look how well just one animal
Fucks up all habitats.

Spring Haiku #1

Desert flowers bloom
Yellow orange purple white
Until the rains end.

Spring Haiku #2

Flowers turn to fruit
Blossoms to berries Blue Straw
Spring to summertime.

Graduation Poem

My best advice
On the path of life
No matter which path you choose:
Treat people with kindness,
Do The Right Thing,
And always make sure to be you.

My Style

I'm no style
And all styles at once.
I'm no smiles
And all smiles at once.
I'm no thought
And all thoughts at once.
I'm no self
And all self at once.
I'm no war
And war on all fronts.

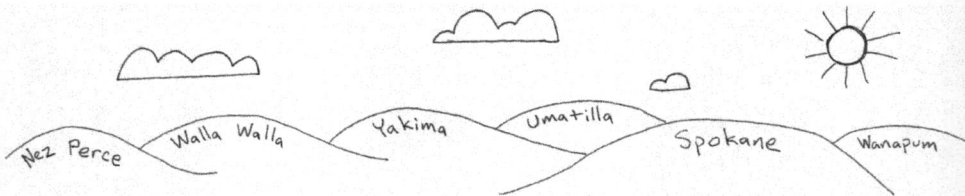

Gentrification 1850

Kill buffalo so we can take land
From native folk, that was the plan
Of the American man in the Nineteenth Century
Manifest Destiny like thats how its meant to be.

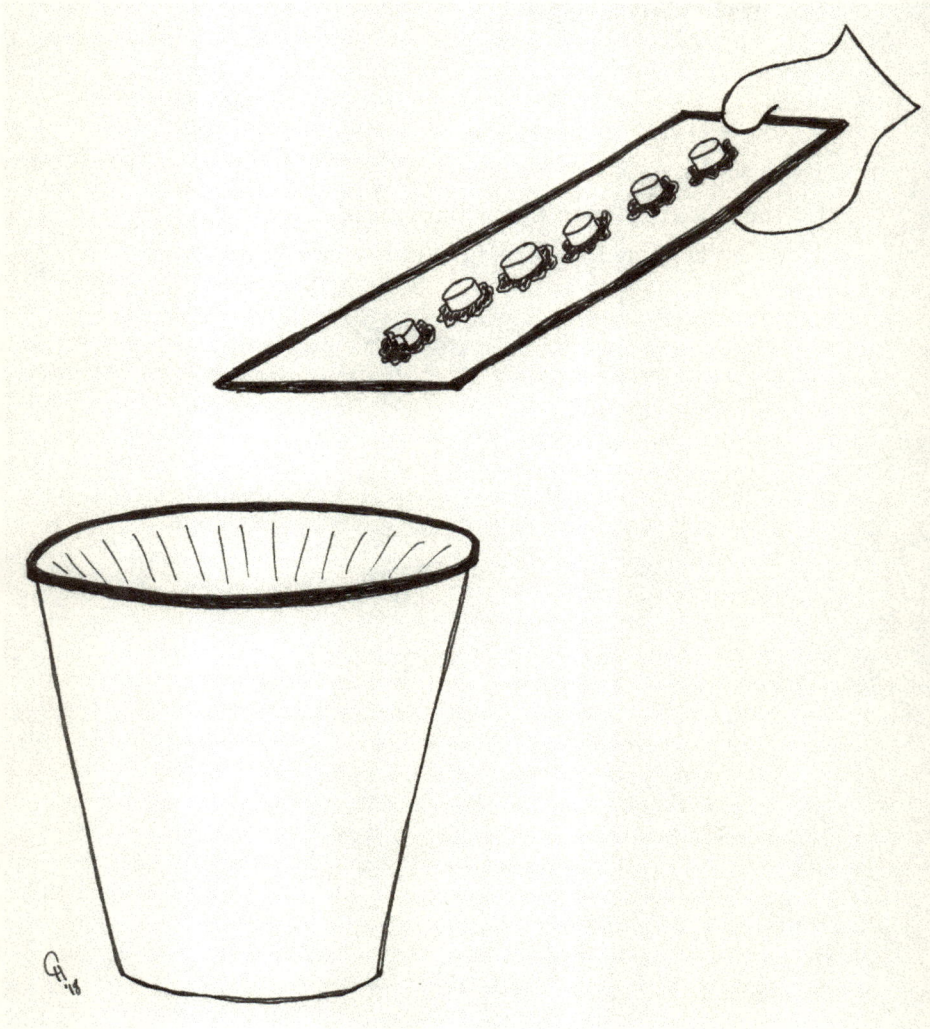

You Gonna Finish That?

How insensitive are we?
How cold must our hearts be?
When 1 in 5 kids in this land
Right now
Could be chronically hungry.
In the world's most obese country
Global leader in food waste
Where we order a platter
Just for a taste.

All The Way Down

I'm down with the God
Cause the God is inside.
I'm down with the God
Cause the God tells me what's right.
I'm down with the God
Cause the God shows me the light.
I'm down with the God
Cause the Gods there every night.

I'm down with the Devil
Cause the Devils inside.
I'm down with the Devil
Cause the Devil can't hide.
I'm down with the Devil
Cause the Devils tried and he's tried.
I'm down with the Devil
Cause it's a hell of a ride.

Big Game

What magnificent animals.
What beauty, what majesty,
What power, what grace.
Masters of their domain,
Kings of the open range.
I love animals so much
And I want to love them all,
So I trap them in a cage
Or kill 'em
And hang them on my wall.

Daddy's Dungeon

I'm unable to submit myself
For sacrifice upon the altar of the mouse,
It's what it is.

The monetary offering necessary to reach the altar
Has made sacrifice by hantavirus
Cost prohibitive.

Plus the crowds, I'm not into it.
If I'm going to drop
The payment for a house
Being sacrificed to a mouse
I don't want to wait in a line all day to do it.

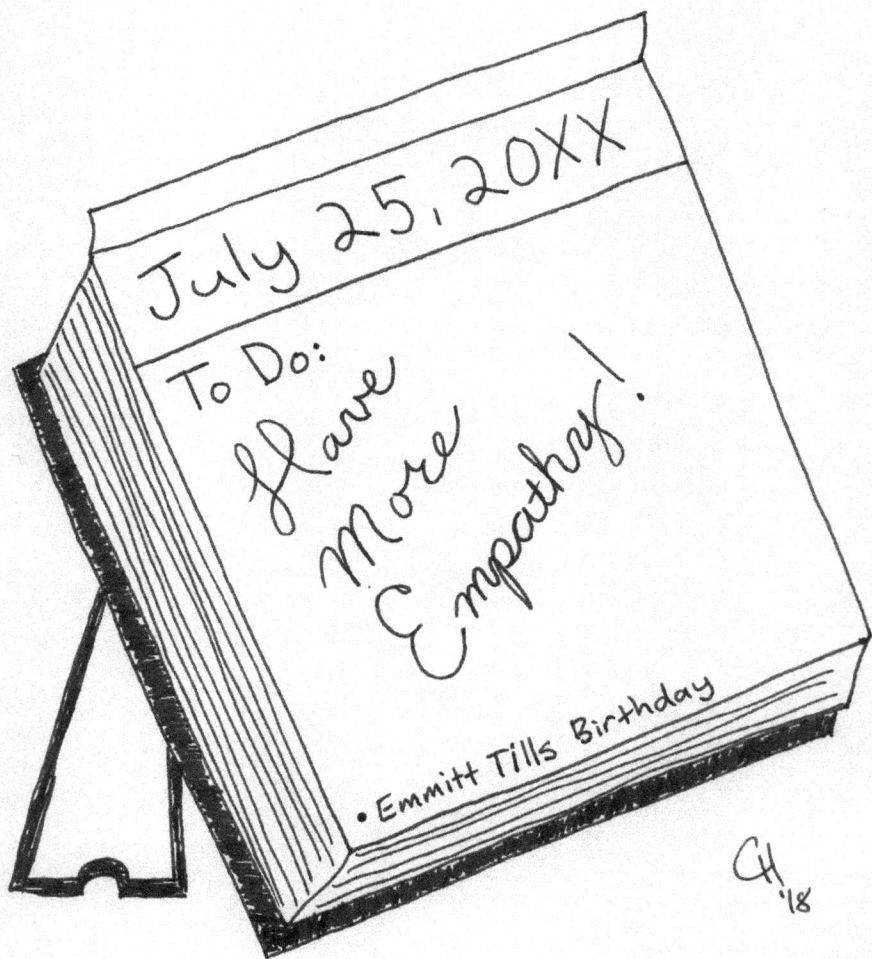

Christmas in July

Why is it that peace
And goodwill toward man
Are only fashionable once a year?
So when the holidays are over
That goodwill disappears.
And peace is just a theory
Or some kind of ideal.
While war and greed and hunger
Are what is really real.
In all the other months
From January to November
You can still be kind to your fellow man
I'd just like you to remember.

Holiday Leftovers

want want want
buy buy buy
wrap wrap wrap
gift gift gift
unwrap unwrap unwrap
play
trash trash trash trash trash
trash trash trash trash trash
trash trash trash trash trash
trash trash trash trash trash
trash trash trash trash trash
trash trash trash trash trash
trash trash trash trash trash
trash trash trash trash trash
trash trash trash trash trash
trash trash trash trash trash
trash trash trash trash trash
trash trash trash trash trash

trash trash trash trash trash
trash trash trash trash trash
trash trash trash trash trash
trash trash trash trash trash
trash trash trash trash trash
trash trash trash trash trash
trash trash trash trash trash
trash trash trash trash trash
trash trash trash trash trash
trash trash trash trash trash
trash trash trash trash trash
trash trash trash trash trash
trash trash trash trash trash
trash trash trash trash trash
trash trash trash trash trash
trash trash trash trash trash
trash trash trash trash trash

G Dubb

George W. Bush!
G Dubb had oil on his face
Like Michael Corleone had the map of Sicily.
Why we all couldn't see it
To me was the real mystery.
Hidden in the sand
Weapons of mass destruction.
Texas contractors got rich
Through Iraqi reconstruction.

Funnel black gold over,
Defend our way of life,
Silence all the critics,
Send flags to all the wives.
DC is full of puppets
Big business pulls the strings.
Push policies to make them rich
Pass the cost to you and me.

Ode to Cardinal Bernard Law

Oh how I'd love to be on that jury
When the saints go marching in,
Perp-walking shackled
Through the courtroom's pearly gates
To face all their victims.

Will saints answer for their sins
Of abusing little kids?
Or are they absolved by hollow oaths taken
About how a saint is supposed to live?

Chickens

What if I said that on 9/11,
Some chickens came home to roost?
Would that be unpatriotic,
Or just plain uncouth?
Or is it just a little truth to power?
Next time they do it
Probably knock down Trump Tower.

Free People (for Leonard & Mumia)

We refuse to be
Tamed or caged.
We refuse to be
Shackled or chained.
You can lock up a body
But can't capture a mind,
No matter how well
Your prisons designed.

Chopper

Everybody send thoughts
Everybody pray,
And keep on doing nothing
Every single day.
Freedoms not an AK
Freedoms not an AR
Freedoms not an M-16
Or a snub .38,
All that they are
Are tools thats
Built for killing,
But killing
Don't make you free.
You're free when
You become willing
To not chop down
The tree.

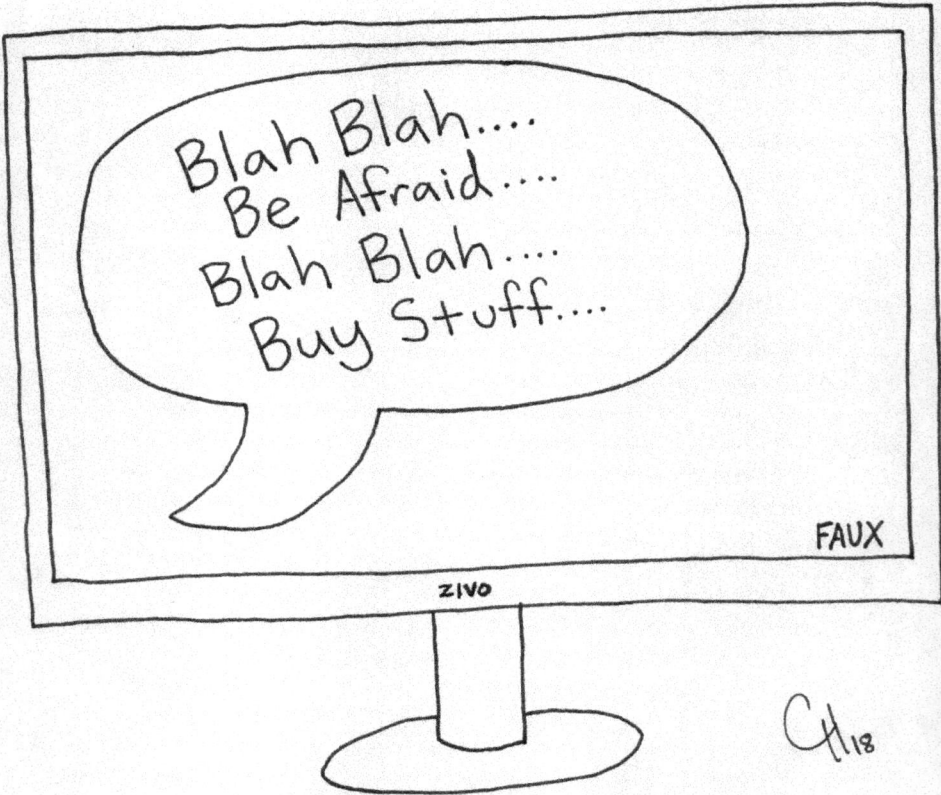

The Overlord's Prayer

Our Patriarch who art in office,
Hypocritical be thine name.
Let thy colonialism come,
So capitalism can be done,
On Earth and also the Heavens.
Give us this day our daily Kool-Aid.
And forgive us of our sins,
As we condemn those who sin against us.
Lead us not into critical thinking,
Because free minds are evil.
For thine is the Empire, and the Authority,
And the Infallible Magnificence, for ever and ever,
Or until it's convenient, or profitable for us to change.
                    Amen.

Ode to the SRO (School Resource Officer)

Four out of six minutes of gunfire you survived
All because you decided to simply stay outside.
While innocents died and bled out on the floor
That's why I now christen you Chickenshit, nothing more.
You didn't go through the door but secured the westside
While inside the hallways of Building 12 bullets flied.
Marjory Stoneman Douglas High was where you failed your test.
Bet the kids there wish they'd had your bulletproof vest.
And I bet you wish you had half the courage of the survivors,
Yet somehow someway they get painted as liars,
While you had the badge the tools and the training.
This here is a pit, go ahead start explaining,
That now 17 dead,
For your inaction, how many on your head?
A Sheriff of Broward
Exposed as a coward instead.

Outro

Thanks for reading, I hope you enjoyed the book! This was my first collection of poems and sketches. Growing up near Seattle and attending Robert Frost Elementary School I was familiar with the road less traveled by, but after graduation I attended the Langston Hughes Finishing School and adopted his stated Motto along the way. I write simple poems because I don't want the reader to wonder what the fuck I'm writing about, and have to spend all of their mental effort having to think about what my poem means. I want the poem's meaning to be pretty clear, and to make the reader think about themselves or something else. So please don't read a bunch of crazy shit into them.

At first I just wrote these for myself because it was fun. After a while I started to feel about them like Raekwon did about the 36 Chambers album, that I "got something that I know everybody wanna hear, cause I know I been waiting to hear it". So now I'm here sharing them and we'll see how it turns out. Peace.

Hit me up and let me know what you think on Twitter
@CarlosHustle509
All Inquiries: motherhubbardcreative@gmail.com or
nonchalantcharlie@gmail.com

Acknowledgments

The author would also like to thank the editor and board of *Tumbleweird Magazine* for first publishing the poems specified under the pen name @CarlosHustle509 :

"Big Game" & "Parental Advisory"	November 2017
"Thinkers" & "Mental Archery"	December 2017
"Bigger, Better, Faster, Cheaper", "God Bless US" &	
"Ode to Cardinal Bernard Law"	January 2018
"Next-Ex" & "Start Your Engines"	February 2018
"Seven Layer Life"	March 2018
"Chopper" & "Earth Day Limerick"	April 2018
"The Overlord's Prayer" & "Spring Haiku #1 & #2"	May 2018